Let's Go Outdoors!

LET'S DIG IN THE GARDEN

By Tina Benjamin

Gareth Stevens PUBLISHING

Please visit our website, www.garethstevens.com. For a free color catalog of all our high-quality books, call toll free 1-800-542-2595 or fax 1-877-542-2596.

Library of Congress Cataloging-in-Publication Data

Benjamin, Tina, author.
Let's dig in the garden / Tina Benjamin.
pages cm. — (Let's go outdoors!)
Includes index.
ISBN 978-1-4824-2613-7 (pbk.)
ISBN 978-1-4824-2614-4 (6 pack)
ISBN 978-1-4824-2615-1 (library binding)
1. Gardening—Juvenile literature. I. Title. II. Series: Let's go outdoors!
SB457.B46 2015
635—dc23
2014049865

First Edition

Published in 2016 by
Gareth Stevens Publishing
111 East 14th Street, Suite 349
New York, NY 10003

Copyright © 2016 Gareth Stevens Publishing

Editor: Ryan Nagelhout
Designer: Nick Domiano

Photo credits: Cover, pp. 1, 15 Ermolaev Alexander/Shutterstock.com; p. 5 Jamie Hooper/Shutterstock.com; p. 7 auremar/Shutterstock.com; p. 9 Loren L. Masseth/Shutterstock.com; pp. 11, 24 (seeds) Denis and Yulia Progostins/Shutterstock.com; pp. 13, 24 (shovel) Naruden Boonareesirichai/Shutterstock.com; p. 17 V. J. Matthew/Shutterstock.com; pp. 19, 24 (watering can) Ditty_about_summer/Shutterstock.com; p. 21 Hellen Grig/Shutterstock.com; p. 23 mast3r/Shutterstock.com.

All rights reserved. No part of this book may be reproduced in any form without permission in writing from the publisher, except by a reviewer.

Printed in the United States of America

CPSIA compliance information: Batch #CS15GS: For further information contact Gareth Stevens, New York, New York at 1-800-542-2595.

Contents

I love my garden!

HERBS

My mom helps me plant.

We have lots
of pumpkins!

They start as tiny seeds.

I have a shovel.
I use it to dig.

I dig out any rocks.

I use gloves.
These keep
my hands clean.

I water my plants.
I use a watering can.

My dad plants herbs.

He uses them to cook!

Words to Know

seeds

shovel

watering can

Index